USBORNE S0-AYX-770
Level Three

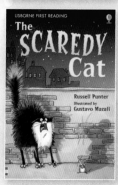  

For more titles in this series, go to
www.usborne.com

Polar Bears

Conrad Mason

Illustrated by
Daniel Howarth

Reading Consultant: Alison Kelly
Roehampton University

Polar bears live near the North Pole.

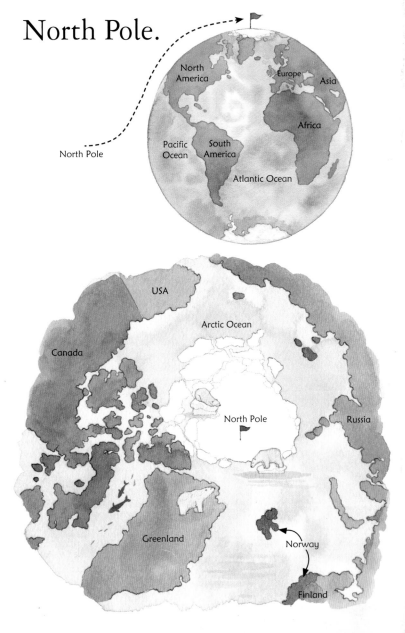

North Pole

North America

Europe

Asia

Africa

Pacific Ocean

South America

Atlantic Ocean

USA

Arctic Ocean

Canada

North Pole

Russia

Greenland

Norway

Finland

There is ice everywhere.

It is very cold, but polar bears stay warm. Their fur keeps them snug.

They even have furry feet.

They have black skin under their fur.

Their tongues are black, too.

They have a thick coat of fat, called blubber.

This makes some grown-up bears as heavy as ten people.

Sometimes a polar bear
gets too hot.

It rubs its tummy in snow,

or jumps into icy water.

Polar bears are good at swimming. They paddle with their front paws,

and steer with their back paws.

8

They poke their head out
of the water to breathe.

Air is trapped in the
bear's fur. This helps
it float, just like a
lifejacket.

9

A polar bear shakes itself like a dog to dry off.

Then it rolls in the snow
to get off the last few drops.

11

Polar bears can climb
up slopes...

jump across gaps...

and step carefully on thin ice.

Their paws
have bumpy
pads that grip
the ice. This
stops them from slipping.

13

They might look cuddly, but polar bears are deadly hunters. They like to eat seals best.

Their white fur makes
them hard to spot.

They have
strong, sharp
teeth, and claws
like daggers.

15

Polar bears hunt on their own.

Sometimes they plod across the ice for days to find seals.

The bear finds a breathing hole. This is a place where seals come up to breathe.

Then it lies in wait.

Sometimes it waits
for hours.

Sometimes it waits for days.

At last, a seal pops out.

Seal for supper!

21

Sometimes a polar bear spots a seal resting. It crawls along the ground, closer...

and closer. It hides behind blocks of ice.

The seal turns around.
The bear stays still.

Then it pounces.

In the summer, some of the ice melts. It's hard to find seals.

Instead, polar bears eat seaweed, moss and berries.

They eat fish and dead seabirds too, and almost anything else they can find.

Some even walk into towns
and hunt for food in dumps.

But they can live for months without any food at all.

Their blubber gives them all the energy they need.

In spring, polar bears get together to become parents.

Sometimes male bears fight over female bears.

They stand up to look big
and scary. They wrestle...

but they don't usually hurt
each other.

29

Polar bear parents stay together for just a few days.

Then they set off on their own again.

In the early winter, the
female bear makes
a den.

This is a cave in the snow,
where her cubs will be born.

31

She chooses a snowy slope,
and starts digging with her
front paws.

She digs a tunnel...

and a cave...

and curls up to sleep.

33

Snow covers the way into the den.

Weeks pass.

In the dead of winter, the mother gives birth to two or three cubs.

Each cub is smaller than a cat. It is born blind, with no teeth.

It clings to its mother, and she feeds it milk.

As weeks pass, the cubs open their shiny black eyes. They grow thick white fur.

The cubs love to play.
They wrestle...

chase each other...

and explore the den.

39

In spring, it's time for
the cubs to leave the den.
Their mother digs the
way out.

The cubs see daylight for the very first time.

Their mother teaches the cubs how to hunt, and how to keep clean.

They roll in snow and go swimming.

This keeps their fur white.
Now they won't be seen when
they hunt.

After about two years, the cubs are almost fully grown. They have learned all that their mother can teach them. It's time to leave.

They may never see her again.

They set off on their own,
to explore the icy world
around them.

Index

Polar bears in trouble

Polar bears are in danger of dying out. Some people hunt them for their fur or meat. But a bigger problem is global warming. The air is slowly getting hotter, which is causing the polar bears' icy home to melt away. Scientists think that there are only around 20,000 polar bears left in the world.

Polar bear websites

You can find out more about polar bears by going to the Usborne Quicklinks Website at www.usborne-quicklinks.com and typing in the keywords "first reading polar bears". Then click on the link for the website you want to visit.

Internet Guidelines

The recommended websites are regularly reviewed and updated but, please note, Usborne Publishing is not responsible for the content of any website other than its own. We recommend that young children are supervised while on the internet.

Designed by Emily Bornoff
Series editor: Lesley Sims
Series designer: Russell Punter
Consultant: Lynn Rogers, Ph.D.
Produced in consultation with the North American Bear Center, Ely, Minnesota, USA
Acknowledgements
Corbis p46 (Hans Strand)

First published in 2009 by Usborne Publishing Ltd., Usborne House, 83-85 Saffron Hill, London EC1N 8RT, England. www.usborne.com
Copyright © 2009 Usborne Publishing Ltd.

USBORNE FIRST READING
Level Four

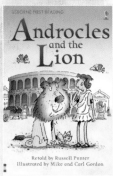

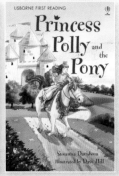